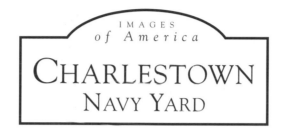

IMAGES
of America

CHARLESTOWN
NAVY YARD

Two unidentified men stand at the center of a propulsion motor stator rewound by the Electric Shop (Building 197) in the 1950s. [BOSTS-14958]

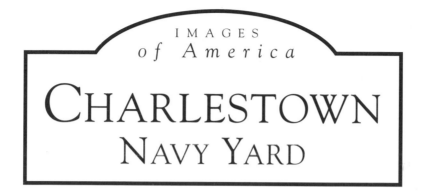

IMAGES
of America

CHARLESTOWN
NAVY YARD

Barbara A. Bither
and Boston National Historical Park

ARCADIA

Published by Arcadia Publishing,
an imprint of Tempus Publishing, Inc.
2 Cumberland Street
Charleston, SC 29401

Printed in Great Britain.

Library of Congress Catalog Card Number:

For all general information contact Arcadia Publishing at:
Telephone 843-853-2070
Fax 843-853-0044
E-Mail edit@arcadiaimages.com

For customer service and orders:
Toll-Free 1-888-313-BOOK

Visit us on the internet at http://www.arcadiaimages.com

The small seaplane tender USS *Humboldt* (AVP-21) slides down Shipways 1 into Boston Harbor on March 17, 1941. [BOST-11455]

CONTENTS

9684—Navy Yard, Boston. Sept 25 1929. US Frigate Constitution

The frigate USS *Constitution*, long associated with the Charlestown Navy Yard, sits in Dry Dock 1 during its extensive restoration in the late 1920s. The Bunker Hill Monument rises in the distance, while the Commandant's House (Quarters G), with awnings and two grand staircases, is just to the left of the dock. Building 22 (which now houses the USS Constitution Museum) and Building 24 are to the right. This area of the yard is now preserved by the National Park Service as part of Boston National Historical Park. [BOSTS-10748]

INTRODUCTION

Deep within Boston Harbor, Charlestown Navy Yard* was birthplace, repair center, outfitting base, and port of refuge for thousands of United States naval vessels. Through photographs and captions, this volume will tell the story of the yard in the 20th century, the ships it served, and the people who kept them seaworthy.

The Charlestown Navy Yard served the U.S. Navy for 174 years from its establishment in 1800 until its closing in 1974. Although the yard produced warships, it was also widely known for its supply and repair functions and for its leadership in technical innovation. This prominence began with the construction of shiphouses that allowed vessels to be built or repaired in any weather, the first naval dry dock in New England, and a ropewalk that provided cordage to the Navy until after World War II. In the 20th century, the yard was responsible for the development of die-lock chain, sonar, missilery, and sophisticated electronics. Many of the images in this volume document these developments and manufacturing processes.

World War II was the high point for the Charlestown Navy Yard. Conservative estimates indicate that between 1939 and 1945 the yard built, repaired, overhauled, converted, or outfitted some 6,000 vessels. The yard work force reached its overall peak of 50,000 during the war.

Increasing reliance on private ship repair yards and shrinking naval appropriations led to the reduction of the Navy's own yards, and in 1973 the Navy announced that the Charlestown Navy Yard was to close.

In 1974 Congress established Boston National Historical Park, which includes 30 acres of the historic Charlestown Navy Yard. The remaining 100 acres continue to be developed as part of the revitalization of Boston's waterfront. The yard today offers visitors a captivating glimpse into the activities that for nearly two centuries supported the United States Navy. Here on the home front, thousands of civilian workers and naval personnel built, repaired, and supplied warships from the majestic sailing vessels of the 19th century to the powerful steel navy of the 20th century.

---

*Although the current name Charlestown Navy Yard has been in common use since the yard's establishment, the facility was officially known as the Boston Navy Yard until November 1945, when it became the Boston Naval Shipyard. For consistency, Charlestown Navy Yard has been used throughout this book.

Two venerable warships, the 1797 frigate USS *Constitution*—the oldest commissioned ship in the Navy—and the powerful 1943 destroyer USS *Cassin Young*, float alongside the working piers, illustrating the changing United States Navy. Both *Constitution*, an active-duty naval vessel, and *Cassin Young,* maintained by National Park Service employees and volunteers, offer free tours daily.

The National Park Service handbook, *Charlestown Navy Yard,* is a lavishly illustrated historical narrative of the yard. Exhibits and tours of the yard provide visitors with opportunities to explore the history of the site and to view buildings, docks, and piers that reflect the yard's 174-year history. One dramatic example is Dry Dock 1, used by USS *Constitution* as early as 1833 and as late as 1995. The USS Constitution Museum, open to visitors daily, offers a rich collection of artifacts, paintings, and models related to the history of "Old Ironsides."

The adaptive reuse of the historic Charlestown Navy Yard has been a highly successful project of the National Park Service, working in partnership with other public agencies and private organizations. This photo history book provides many views of the 20th-century yard, evoking a time when the Charlestown Navy Yard was a major industrial facility proudly serving the United States Navy.

Pipe Shop (Shop 56) employees pose for the camera during an unknown event in the early 1950s. They typify the thousands of men and women who worked at the yard through its long history. [BOSTS-7774]

THE PHOTOGRAPHERS

After the Charlestown Navy Yard closed in 1974, the Navy transferred considerable historical material to the National Park Service, including a collection of 80,000 black-and-white prints, glass and film negatives, slides, and albums. In the late 1980s, Boston National Historical Park began cataloging this collection, which forms the basis of this book; the catalog number of each image appears in brackets at the end of its caption.

Most of the images were taken in the 20th century by official yard photographers. Prior to the arrival of Harry C. Berry, the first identified official photographer, the Navy had documented demolition and construction of buildings as it modernized the yard to service steel vessels. In addition to documenting changes in the yard's physical appearance, the photographic staff recorded official events and workers' activities, often in response to requests from the yard's Public Affairs Office or the shipyard newspaper. Official events included ceremonies such as christenings, commissionings, and changes of command, while workers' activities ranged from ship repair to manufacturing; even employee recreational events were the subject of the cameraman's lens.

In May 1923 Howell Baldwin replaced Berry as official photographer. Under him, the photographic operation grew until, by World War II, 17 employees worked in the Photo Lab. As supervisor, Baldwin oversaw taking and processing photographs; a blueprint facility; photomacrographic equipment in the Materials Lab; and x-ray and gamma-ray photography, used in inspecting such items as forgings and castings, in the Radiographic Lab.

From 1923 to 1974, the photo supervisors included Baldwin, Stanley P. Mixon, George A. Moran, and John (Jack) W. Doherty. Others who worked in the lab included Dennis Costin, Paul E. Feeney, Stanley Kaplan, John F. Lemis, Nicholas J. Metta, John N. Moore, Robert M. Snow, and Walter J. Zakszewski. Images taken by Costin, Doherty, Kaplan, Metta, and Mixon appear in this book, with their names listed before the catalog number of the image where applicable.

The individual photographers came from a variety of backgrounds. Baldwin held a degree from the Syracuse University College of Photography, had worked as a newspaper photographer, and was a U.S. Army aerial photographer during World War I. Nicholas Metta had been an aerial photographer in the Army Air Corps during World War II and had survived the Bataan Death March following his capture by the Japanese in the Philippines. He came to the yard as a helper machinist in March 1952, transferring to the Photo Lab in December 1952.

Jack Doherty, the last supervisor, also had a background as a combat photographer. Hired as a woodworker, he transferred to the Photo Lab in 1949 and became supervisor in 1965. The last employee in the Photo Lab, Robert Snow, started his career as a welder at the South Boston Annex, working on projects such as the 1959–1962 conversion of USS *Albany*. After the yard closed, Snow continued to work for the First Naval District as a photographer until his retirement in 1982.

The photographers primarily worked in Buildings 34 and 39, sharing space with many other functions. Building 34 housed the Photo and Metallurgical Labs, while Building 39 housed the blueprint room and contained a photostat and fotoform camera. In 1941 Building 5 contained a photo identification unit, also a part of the lab.

On July 24, 1969, Jack Doherty caught fellow members of the Photo Lab photographing carpenter stoppers being tested in the Forge Shop (Building 105). Stanley Kaplan (right) checks a movie camera on a tripod in a test pit as lighting preparations are completed. The light stand is part of a carpenter stopper turned on its side. [BOSTS-7744]

SOURCES AND ACKNOWLEDGMENTS

Resources consulted in the original cataloging of the photographs and in the writing of this volume were many and varied. Key sources were the archival records of the yard's Public Affairs Office in the Boston National Historical Park collection and Navy Yard records at the National Archives—New England Division, Waltham, Massachusetts, as well as a complete run of the shipyard newspaper, *Boston Navy Yard News* (after 1945, *Boston Naval Shipyard News*), in the park archives.

Oral history interviews conducted by the staff of Boston National Historical Park with individuals who either lived in or were employed by the Navy Yard greatly enhanced understanding the human side of the yard. Subjects of these interviews included Admiral and Mrs. Raymond Burk, Lyman Carlow, Allan R. Crite, Mary Doherty, Barbara Tuttle Green, David Himmelfarb, Paul Ivas, John Langan, Fred Meade, Kenneth J. Mitchell, Robert M. Snow, Helen Walsh, Evelyn Williams, Frances Williams, and Susan Williams.

Official histories of the yard include George O.Q. Mansfield's *Historical Review: Boston Naval Shipyard, 1938–1957* (1957); Frederick R. Black's *Charlestown Navy Yard, 1890–1973* (1988); and Steve Carlson's *Ships Built by the Charlestown Navy Yard* (draft, 1992). Mary Pat Kelly's article, "The Mason Comes Home" (*American Legacy*, vol. 2 no. 1 [Spring 1996]), provided valuable information on the crew of the USS *Mason*.

Barbara Bither and Boston National Historical Park gratefully wish to acknowledge the assistance of several individuals who helped to make this book possible. We want to thank the following from the National Park Service: Phil Bergen, Marty Blatt, Steve Carlson, Arsen Charles, Mike Gibson, Phil Hunt, Louis Hutchins, Ruth Raphael, Dave Rose, Gay Vietzke, and Paul Weinbaum. Student Conservation Association interns David Dobmeyer and Tim Bingaman provided valuable assistance, as did Jack Green, Charles Haberlein, and Mark Wertheimer of the Naval Historical Center, Washington, D.C.

Although ship activity had moderated since the end of World War II, it is still very much in evidence in this *c.* 1949 view. USS *LST-1154* (later named *Tallahatchie County*) is in Dry Dock 2 at the center of the photograph, possibly during its post-shakedown inspection. Buildings 195, 197, and 42 dominate the area to the right of Dry Dock 2, while the approaches to the Mystic-Tobin Bridge loom just beyond the northern boundary of the yard. This view gives an idea of the look of the yard at the time the U.S. Navy turned the property over to the National Park Service and the City of Boston in the mid-1970s. [BOSTS-8619]

One
THE YARD AT A GLANCE

This April 1960 aerial view shows the Charlestown Navy Yard as a vibrant repair facility. It looks west from Pier 11, where the aircraft carrier USS *Wasp* (CVS-18) is docked, toward downtown Boston, where the spire of the Customs House can be seen on the left and the Suffolk County Courthouse on the right. Note floating dry dock *ARD-16* in Dry Dock 5. Moored vessels include USS *Macon* (CA-132) by Pier 9 and USS *Thor* (ARC-4) at Pier 8. [Jack Doherty, BOSTS-10111]

K.K. Najarian and F.A. George photographed this panorama of the Navy Yard during Navy Day celebrations on May 13, 1916. From the far left, where a man stands at the top of the Coal Handling Plant (Building 109), to the far right, where ferries, a steamer, and USS *Henley* (DD-39) ply Boston Harbor, ships line the piers dressed with flags in honor of the day. Basket masts in the background indicate the presence of the battleships of the Third Battle Division of the Atlantic Fleet, based at the yard. The stately masts of USS *Constitution* rise in the middle of

Navy Day Celebration, May 13, 1916, Boston, Mass.

the photograph, while the repair ship USS *Vestal* (AR-4) is in the foreground. The Machine Shop (Building 42), with four large arches reaching above expanses of glass and doors, dominates the background. A chimney and hammerhead cranes appear behind the building, while the Paint Shop (Building 125) can be seen in front of it, to the left. The panorama is celebratory, displaying proudly the build-up of the Navy prior to the nation's entry into World War I. [Krikos Kaspar Najarian, Gift of the Najarian Family]

At the height of World War II, shipbuilders wasted no time in constructing destroyer escorts for Great Britain. Photographed on August 17, 1943, the four partially-completed ships in Dry Dock 5 had been started just three days earlier. Prefabricated sections, such as the bow on the barge (top center), sped up the shipbuilding process. In the background are HMS *Duckworth* (K.351) and USS *Constitution*. [BOSTS-8685]

Large trees line Second Avenue in 1904 as men using wagons and animals pave the street. To the left is the Marine Barracks (Quarters I). [BOSTS-8655]

16

Dated 1872, this view shows the head of Dry Dock 1 looking toward the Commandant's House (Quarters G) and the Bunker Hill Monument. Oxen—the trucks of the 19th century—stand at the dry dock's edge. [BOSTS-8880]

This 1957 aerial view looks northeast into the heart of the yard. USS *Providence* (CL-82), at Pier 5 in the center of the picture, is in the yard for conversion into a guided-missile cruiser. [Edmund Katz, USCG; BOSTS-8619]

The South Boston Annex was located 2 miles across the harbor from the main yard in Charlestown. This 1943 aerial shows the annex at its height during World War II. Dry Dock 3, located to the left of the triangular jetty, was one of the largest on the east coast. USS *Wakefield* (AP-21) can be seen in the background at the far side of Dry Dock 4. [BOSTS-7791]

USS *Wakefield* initiates Dry Dock 4 on April 24, 1943. Employees stand on and next to the caisson as it is seated into the sill, closing off the dock in preparation for draining. The converted passenger liner, which had been seriously damaged by fire, was stripped to the waterline and rebuilt as a troopship. [BOSTS-14604]

By the mid-1950s, the South Boston Annex was used for storage for inactive aircraft carriers of the Atlantic Fleet. This bird's-eye view of the "mothball" fleet looks from Pier 2 at the left to the jetty and Dry Dock 3 at the right. [BOSTS-7793]

In June 1965 USS *Wasp* (CVS-18) lies at the jetty during a port visit, while USS *Shangri-La* (CVS-38) undergoes repairs in Dry Dock 3. Also shown is USS *Boston* (CAG-1). Gone is the inactive fleet, disbanded in the late 1950s. [Ruth Bradshaw, BOSTS-7795]

"Lighting off the first boiler" in January 1967 marked the rebirth of USS *Decatur* (DD-936) as a guided-missile destroyer (DDG-31). This important step toward ship self-sufficiency meant it was no longer dependent on yard resources for power to support shipboard work. On this occasion, Philip A. Ruggiero holds the torch to start the boiler, while Peter Calcagni and Richard E. Black smile at the camera. [BOSTS-10914]

Two
WORKERS ON SHORE

Employees of the Electronics Shop gather to learn about a new radio transceiver. Ed Powers, chief of the shop, is in the center of the photograph wearing a white hard hat. Training was a part of life at the shipyard, from new apprentices to seasoned staff. [BOSTS-7761]

The Navy Yard maintained an active apprenticeship program. "Apprentices worked along with the full mechanics, and as assistants to them," recalled Susan Williams, seen in 1967 crimping lugs onto wires to make an antisubmarine rocket (ASROC) connector plug in the Fire Control Shop (Building 197). "We used to work for three weeks a month and then they'd send us to school for one week." [BOSTS-7373]

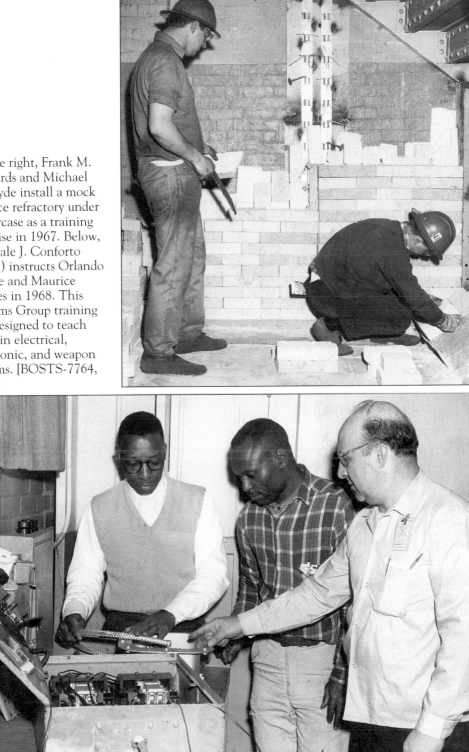

To the right, Frank M. Richards and Michael M. Hyde install a mock furnace refractory under a staircase as a training exercise in 1967. Below, Pasquale J. Conforto (right) instructs Orlando Boone and Maurice Nobles in 1968. This Systems Group training was designed to teach skills in electrical, electronic, and weapon systems. [BOSTS-7764, 7765]

Rope production was one of the oldest manufacturing processes carried out in the Navy Yard. The Boston Ropewalk (Building 58) was constructed so that machines would do the work. "Everything was a production line," recalled Fred Meade. "You were required to do a certain amount of work in an 8-hour day. If you were spinning yarn, you were required to do 130 14-pound bobbins." Some hand work was still necessary, however. Short hemp fibers could not be spun mechanically; hand spinning was instituted to use what would otherwise be waste. Three ropemakers demonstrate hand spinning while a "wheelboy" turns the spinning wheel. [BOSTS-9540]

Opposite: Turning hemp into rope was a multi-stage process that began with hackling (or combing) the hemp fibers to break them apart and form them into parallel rows of fibers known as sliver. The images show this process before and after mechanization. In the top view from the early 20th century, hackling benches and long-toothed combs line the wall by the windows in the Hemp House (Building 62). At bottom, Supervisor John R. Concannon Jr. watches as Charles Callahan and Isadore Yarnetski feed hemp into a breaking machine on the second floor of the Ropewalk (Building 58) in November 1951. [BOSTS-9576, 9544]

U.S. NAVY YARD BOSTON
ROPEWALK BLDG 62
AMERICAN HEMP HACKLING BENCHES

Sliver was spun to make yarn. Barrels of the processed fiber wait at right to be fed into a spinning jenny. A workman checks the sliver while another feeds it into the machine. To the far left, a bobbin takes up the twisted sliver as yarn. The bobbins of yarn were then combined and wound onto a reel at the end of a forming machine. The rope was close to being a finished product. [BOSTS-9544]

Ropemaker Lawrence Post loads a bobbin onto a frame of a forming machine in 1951. The take-up reel is in the foreground. [BOSTS-9544]

Riggers inside Building 24 splice together a piece of 12-inch nylon rope in September 1970. Anthony Vitale is the rigger at the far right, in the background. [BOSTS-9307]

Continuing the sequence from the previous page, the image below depicts the next step in the ropemaking process: the transfer of the take-up reel to a layer used to twist the rope into its final form. Amerigo Colella moves a reel of rope using an overhead hoist and dolly. [BOSTS-9544]

Since Dry Dock 1 was one of two sizeable dry docks in the Boston area, it was extensively used by commercial firms in periods of low U.S. Navy activity. In September 1899 the five-masted schooner *John Prescott* towers majestically over the dock and Buildings 22 and 24. [BOSTS-14957]

Sailmakers cut and assemble sails in the Sail Loft (Building 33) in the 1920s. Yardarms suspended from the ceiling at the center of the room assist in manufacturing individual sails. [BOSTS-9333]

In 1966 the Wyman Gordon Company of Worcester contracted to have the yard unload a 133-ton casting from the Dutch freighter MV *Schiedyk* onto a special railroad car. Here the German-made casting is being lifted from the deck of floating crane *YD-196* onto the flat car. [BOSTS-7728]

The shipyard newspaper heralded advances in shipyard technology with photographs, such as this 1967 view of the Sheetmetal Shop's new numerically controlled turret-punch press. Robert W. Benson and Ernest Benedetto demonstrate the press, which saved time and increased precision by repeatedly punching holes into metal plates—an operation previously done by hand. [BOSTS-7732]

In 1953 a Bliss trimming press (right) was installed in the Forge Shop (Building 105) to trim excess material from forged items such as chain or carpenter stoppers. In the 1966 image above, a worker uses tongs to handle a carpenter stopper during trimming. [Above, Stanley Kaplan, BOSTS-9701; right, BOSTS-9718]

OFFICIAL U. S. NAVY PHOTOGRAPH
Not For Publication Unless Officially Released

Rough Forging being Placed
into Die

EXHIBIT IVc

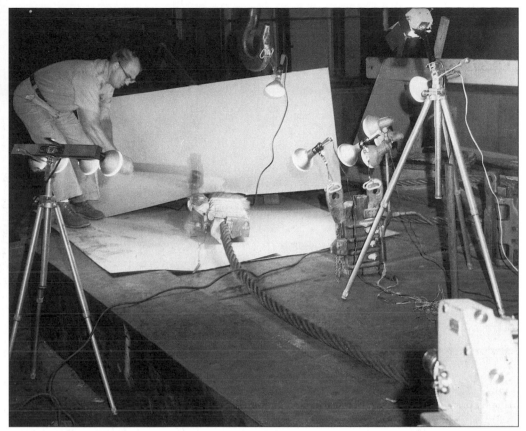

Anchor chain and carpenter stoppers constituted two major products of the Forge Shop. Paul Ivas, master of the shop, recalled that the carpenter stopper—a hold-and-quick-release device for wire-rope used in salvage work, in towing, and for tying down   became a high priority item in early 1966 because of the increased need for salvage equipment for use in Vietnam. In the top image on the opposite page, a rough forging for a carpenter stopper is being placed into a die; in the bottom image, a number of finished stoppers wait on pallets for shipment. On this page, a workman demonstrates the quick release of the carpenter stopper in July 1969; the motion of the hammer is caught by the camera. [Opposite, Stanley Kaplan, BOSTS-9701; above, Jack Doherty, BOSTS-7744]

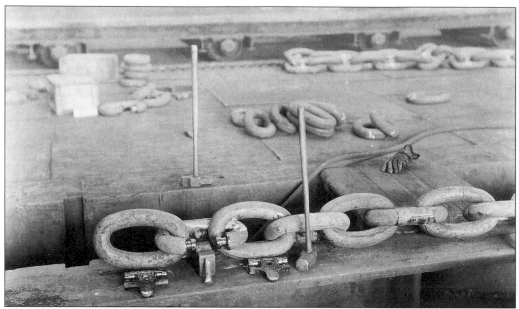

The Navy Yard developed a superior chain by alternating a drop-forged detachable link with a solid link. Such was its reputation that in 1927 the Panama Canal Commission contracted with the yard to produce chain for use on the canal locks. This close-up shows solid-link chain interspersed with detachable links. [BOSTS-9666]

In this early-20th-century view, the furnaces in the Forge Shop are fueled by coal. Chain being assembled hangs suspended from the ceiling, while completed chain lays stretched out on the floor. [BOSTS-9665]

The yard further revolutionized chain manufacturing in the 1920s with the development of die-lock chain. Formed by the mechanical linking of two separate forgings—a stem and socket—die-lock was stronger, more uniform, and cheaper than cast iron or cast steel. In the above view from the 1950s or 1960s, stems lie in a pile before joining with sockets as a drop hammer creates a link. To the right, piles of die-lock chain await shipment in September 1943. [Above, BOSTS-9672; right, BOSTS-9669]

Forger John J. Miller places a hot socket into a cold stem inside the lower half of the die on the drop hammer. Through weight and pressure from the drop, the upper half of the die will bind the two pieces together to form one die-lock chain link. [BOSTS-9672]

In March 1955 the yard completed its largest forging job to date—the manufacture of 4.75-inch die-lock chain as well as the shank and assembly of the anchor for the aircraft carrier USS *Forrestal* (CVA-59). Above, one of Building 105's bridge cranes lowers the 60,000-pound anchor onto a lowboy trailer. At right, the anchor is suspended next to one from USS *Constitution* to compare the change in technology over 160 years. [BOSTS-9690]

Women constituted a sizeable portion of the Charlestown Navy Yard's work force during World War II. Celebrating Forge Shop accomplishments, these women hold the largest and the smallest die-lock chain links produced by the yard for a feature in the August 12, 1944 issue of the shipyard's newspaper. The small link, for .75-inch chain, measures 4.5 inches long and weighs 22 ounces, while the large link, for 3.75-inch chain, measures 24 inches long and weighs 190 pounds. [BOSTS-9669]

Three
THE PHYSICAL PLANT

The Charlestown Navy Yard's shipbuilding facilities boomed during World War II. Two destroyer escorts for Britain—HMS *Bayntun* (K.310) and HMS *Bazely* (K.311)—are under construction in an unfinished Dry Dock 5; cofferdams keep water out while the gate is completed. This image demonstrates the urgency of the times: if the dock was dry and could accommodate a ship, then shipbuilding went on. [BOSTS-8855]

These 1874 or 1875 waterfront views form a panorama of the Navy Yard in the post–Civil War period, an era of little activity. From west (left) to east, visible features include the multi-chimneyed Smith Shop (removed in July 1875); the Carpenters Shop (Building 24); the Dry Dock Pump House (Building 22) with its large chimney; the Tinners and Plumbers Shop (Building 28); the long, arched wall of the yard's battery, with the flagpole and Magazine (Building 48) behind it; the granite Joiners Shop (Building 36); the massive brick facade and high arching windows of the Machine Shop, Foundry, and Smithery (Building 42), partially obscured by temporary waterfront sheds (Buildings 44, 45, 46, and 82); and three shiphouses (Buildings 68, 71, and 73), which allowed construction of ships in all weather. In the distance at left, the Bunker Hill Monument pierces the sky.

To the right of Building 42 are three ships—USS *Wabash*, in the process of being fitted out as the yard's Receiving Ship (temporary barracks), and the stored USS *Niagara* and USS *Ammonoosuc*. The unfinished hull of a steam frigate occupies the shipbuilding ways between the shiphouses. *Niagara*, *Ammonoosuc*, and the unlaunched frigate would be broken up for scrap in the 1880s, but *Wabash* would remain a fixture of the yard's waterfront until 1912. With the exception of the battery, temporary buildings, and shiphouses, all of the buildings seen here remain in the yard today. Their locations can be seen on the yard plans on pp. 122–127. [BOSTS-8639]

Novy Yard Boston S Side Bldg 109 from S.E. Nov. 23 1912   109-20

With the shift from sail to steam power, the ability to provide coal for fuel became increasingly important. In the early 1900s, the Navy constructed a Coaling Plant (Building 109) on Pier 1. In the 1902 view at the top opposite, wooden forms for concrete bulkheads are in place by the edge of the pier, which had to be extensively reconstructed to accommodate the new facility. At bottom, the completed plant is seen. A track for coal cars swoops upward around from the ground on the far side to the roof line on the water side. The building looks serene, but it was a noisy and dirty place during coaling operations. Above, the coaling of a ship is in progress. As an unidentified witness recalled for the shipyard newspaper many years later, this operation could take as long as two days. "About halfway through the first day of coaling, things began to look pretty dark and by the time the job was finished . . . the men, their uniforms, the ship, the dock were covered with a film of finely powdered coal dust." [BOSTS-9807, 9808]

This unique stereograph from the 1860s or 1870s shows a pair of swinging gates closing the end of Dry Dock 1. Installed between 1827 and 1833, the gates sealed the dock while the caisson was being repaired; by 1911 they had been removed. In the view below, three men pose inside the dock close to the site of the former gates. [BOSTS-8789, 8790]

Charlestown annually celebrates the Battle of Bunker Hill with a parade. In 1914 sailors from the Navy Yard march down Chelsea Street past the Commandant's House (Quarters G), seen on the right behind the wall. A gap in the wall allowed access to the house from Chelsea Street through a fenced-in front yard. The Marine Barracks (Quarters I) is in the background. [BOSTS-10085]

Taken between 1897 and 1899, this photograph shows the yard side of Quarters G after a snowstorm. A trellis leads up to the front of the home and a guard house is by the gate. The houses of Charlestown are in the background. The present sun porch on the building was constructed by the Works Progress Administration (WPA) in 1936. [BOSTS-14957]

A major modernization of the Navy Yard's facilities took place in the late 1890s and early 1900s. A monumental gatehouse was a part of this effort. In the 1902 construction view above, Quarters A and B are visible behind the bricklayers. Quarters A, used alternately throughout the 19th century by porters and guards, later housed the docking officer and the assistant planning superintendent. It was torn down in the 1950s. The completed Main Gate (Building 97), shown at top right, was an impressive chess piece. As if its function was not obvious, a sign painted on the wall of the adjoining Building 4 clarified the situation. To the left are Riordan's Stables. Cobblestones pave Wapping Street up to the Main Gate. By 1958, the gate had become a barrier to trucks carrying materials into the yard. It was demolished and replaced by a small Guard House (Building 267). Seen below right in 1971, the brick wall above the Gate 1 sign is all that remains of Riordan's Stables, but cobblestones still pave Wapping Street. [BOSTS-8943, 8949]

2200
NAVY YARD BOSTON
MAIN GATE FROM S.W.
NOV. 26, 1915.

The Marine Barracks (Quarters I) receives a facelift in 1941, one of a number of renovation projects undertaken in the yard by the WPA. Reinforced outdoor porches and two brick fireproof escape towers are under construction. The completed porches can be seen in the photograph on p. 12, at the far left just below the Mystic-Tobin Bridge ramps. [BOSTS-9223]

For many years, private firms provided food service for yard workers. In 1921, Crowley's Restaurant, located in Building 28, had a soda fountain and sold convenience items such as soap, cigarettes, and gum. [BOSTS-9311]

It is lunchtime in this 1952 view of the congested cafeteria located in Building 36. By this time, food service was run as a cooperative by a Civilian Cafeteria Board made up of yard employees. [BOSTS-9360]

In December 1972, the Navy Exchange Service Station (Building 194) on Pier 1 was selling gas for 30¢ per gallon. [BOSTS-15754]

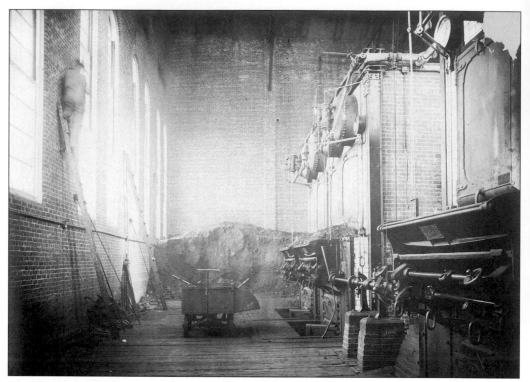

F105 N11
NAVY YARD BOSTON MASS
6-7-1902
BUILDING 105

The headhouse, or front section, of the Forge Shop (Building 105) served as a power plant before all Navy Yard power needs were combined into a single Central Power Plant (Building 108). At top right, the steel skeleton of the Building 105 headhouse surrounds an earlier power plant; a month later, the view at left shows scaffolding for bricklayers in place along the Second Avenue elevation. The completed headhouse was divided into two sections by a brick wall. One half (bottom right) held the generators and a switchboard, while the other (above) housed boilers and coal. A ghostly man can be seen on a ladder by an electric wall sconce. [Left and top right, BOSTS-9643; above and bottom right, BOSTS-9652]

By late 1931, work is under way to convert the headhouse into a roundhouse for the Navy Yard's locomotives and cranes. Above, the foundation and ties for the railroad tracks leading into the building end at the large windows, which were later converted into doors. [BOSTS-9647]

F 66 N9   NAVY YARD BOSTON FEB.1,1903.   BUILDING NO.66   IRON PLATERS' SHOP.

The main portion of the Forge Shop occupied the site of the Iron Platers' Shop (Building 66). Demolition of that structure began in the winter of 1902–1903 (opposite page, bottom image). By the summer of 1903 (top image, this page) the work had progressed to the point where there was a clear view of the newly completed Metal Workers Shop, Galvanizing Plant, and Central Tool Room (Building 106). By early 1904 (above), brickwork for Building 105 along First Avenue was complete. In the background looms the steel skeleton for the rest of the structure. [BOSTS-9581, 9643]

Even as the yard modified and replaced its facilities, work continued unabated. John O'Brien and Doug Ginsberg pour liquid aluminum into molds for 2.25-inch chain inside the Foundry (Building 42). [BOSTS-9450]

Opposite: These views of the reconstruction of the sea wall between Piers 6 and 7 give a rare glimpse into the yard during World War II. It was a busy work site where employees were concerned not as much with how things were done as with results and moving the war toward conclusion. In the earlier view at the bottom, a destroyer or destroyer escort is being fitted out at a nearby pier. In the top view, looking in the opposite direction, wooden scaffolding indicates new ship construction on Shipways 1 and 2. A corner of Building 42 is at left. [BOSTS-15663, 8745]

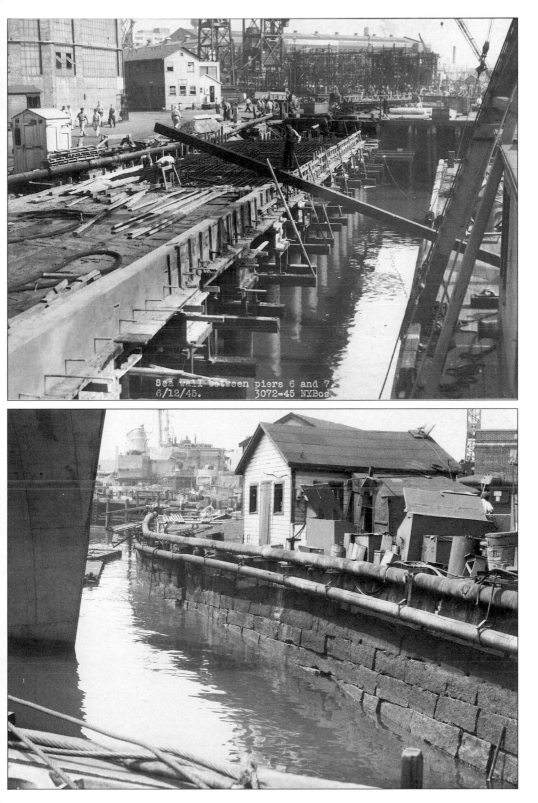

Sea wall between piers 6 and 7.
6/12/45.   3072-45 NYBos.

With booms reaching skyward, portal cranes were shipyard landmarks for most of the 20th century. Portal Crane 19 is being used to test the condition of the crane rail foundations on the east side of Dry Dock 2. Test weights hang suspended from the crane's boom. Building 195, now the site of Shipyard Park, is at right, as is a portion of the circular Pump House (Building 123) for Dry Docks 1 and 2. [BOSTS-8840]

Two workers sit on a board in a crane rail test pit. Boots are a required part of their work uniform. [BOSTS-8840]

A Mark-13 guided-missile launcher assembly for use on the guided-missile destroyer USS *Decatur* (DDG-31) is being lowered into or raised out of a temporary shelter on Pier 5. Covered barge *YFN-302* can be seen behind the shelter. [BOSTS-10897]

F40IN229   NAVY YARD BOSTON DEC 1 1904   DRY DOCK 2

Two separate photographs taken the same day link together at the east wall of Dry Dock 2 to form a panorama. Construction of Dry Dock 2 began in 1899 on the site of a former Timber Basin and was completed in 1905, when the armored cruiser USS *Maryland* became the first ship to test the dock. The photographer stands on an earthen cofferdam (part of which can be

F401N230 NAVY YARD BOSTON, DEC 1 1904 DRY DOCK 2

seen in the image on the right) built to restrain harbor waters during dock construction. To the right of Building 42 are two remnants of the pre-1900 Navy Yard battery—a heavy shell house and a small hexagonal magazine. Split between the two images is the circular Dry Dock Pump House (Building 123). [BOSTS-8808]

Dry Dock 2 was one of the largest construction projects ever undertaken at Charlestown. The three progress views on these two pages document the work. At top opposite, the skyline of Boston can be seen behind the wood cribbing for the cofferdam that sealed off the construction site. The steeple of Old North Church is at the center. Removal of over 250,000 cubic yards of material from the site was slowed by three collapses of this dam. Buildings 24, 22, and 28 are visible in the view above, which was taken shortly after the third collapse. In the photo at bottom opposite, lines from shears (hoists) criss-cross the site. Over 11,200 granite blocks went into the structure. [BOSTS-8808]

Dock No.2. Boston.   Coffer Dam from East End.   Nov. 18, 1899

F4D N227   NAVY YARD BOSTON MAY 2 1904   DRY DOCK NO.2

In the late 1940s renovations resolved settling problems with the outer section of Dry Dock 2. Above, a man sits on an I-beam used in the formation of cells built to restrain harbor waters during the work. The Electronics Shop (Building 197) is behind him. Below, thick cables pass like snakes around an electrician working on improved electrical service. [BOSTS-8816, 8817]

The octagonal Muster House (Building 31) was built in the 1850s as a place for employees to gather to receive work assignments each morning. By the time the view above was taken in 1904, employees no longer mustered daily; the unique building housed the yard's telephone exchange, a chemical laboratory, and offices for the captain of the yard. Below, the structure's porch frames USS *Utah* (BB-31) sitting in Dry Dock 2 in the late 1920s. Tennis courts occupy the space between the Muster House and the ship. [BOSTS-9316, 14516]

NAVY YARD, BOSTON.
PUBLIC WORKS OFFICES, BLDG. 107
FEB.11, 1921. FROM W.
5784

These two images show the exterior and interior of the Public Works Shop (Building 107). Projecting from the dormer is a tray used to develop blueprints utilizing sunlight. The building continues in its original function today as Boston National Historical Park's maintenance facility. [BOSTS-9751]

NAVY YARD, BOSTON.
PUBLIC WORKS DRAFTING ROOM, BLDG. 107
FEB.11, 1921.
5786

Since hemp used in ropemaking was flammable, a fire could be devastating. This view of Building 96 was taken two days after a fire blazed through the structure. If the 1939 view below inside Building 77 is any indication of how hemp was stored, it is a wonder that there was not more damage. [BOSTS-9600, 9595]

The views on these two pages show changes to the east end of the Navy Yard prior to World
War I. In the view above, spectators view the charred ruins of the Spar Shed (Building 85)
following a fire in 1900. The Little Mystic Channel Bridge arches over the remains. Within
three years, a new Sawmill and Spar Shed (Building 114) rose on the site. That building, which
later became the Boat Shop, can be seen to the right in the top view of a motor dory being
tested in the Timber Basin. Like its contemporaries, it was of brick construction, contrasting
with the granite Timber Shed (Building 76) and Mold Loft (Building 77) of an earlier day at
left. The wing of Building 114 at center was removed in the 1990s to accommodate a new road
access, Gate 6. The Timber Basin was drained around 1913 to allow construction of a fuel-oil
tank. In the bottom image on the opposite page, the Navy combined two separate photographs
of this area to create a panorama showing the reinforcement steel for the entire tank floor.
Building 114 is in the center background, with the Little Mystic Channel Bridge and Mystic
Pier to the right. [BOSTS-10048, 14914, 8987]

21 FT. MOTOR DORY.

NAVY YARD BOSTON

APRIL 25. 1911

NAVY YARD BOSTON

FUEL OIL TANK FROM ==

DEC 15. 1912 DAY LABOR 514 B

514-5A

Logs float in the remnant of the Timber Basin in this view of 16th Street looking toward East Boston. A newly completed Storehouse (Building 131) is at center, while the Metalworkers Shop (Building 106) and a Timber Shed (Building 75) are at right. [BOSTS-8662]

Following construction of Dry Dock 2, the Receiving Ship USS *Wabash* moved to the foot of 16th Street at the far east end of the yard. [BOSTS-14574]

Master Boat Builder Robertson (1) is among the men conducting a floatation and stability test of a dory in 1908. USS *Wabash* and the edge of land forming the Timber Basin are in the background. [BOSTS-14914]

Looking in the opposite direction from the view on p. 68, pipes for drains on 16th Street are stacked at right. On the west side of the street are Buildings 75, 76, and 77. [BOSTS-8662]

REPLACEMENT PIER #11

REPLACEMENT PIER #11
NOV-85264   TYPICAL CONCRETE DECK POUR   NY2-4073(L)7-19-56

Thirteen years after its original construction, Pier 11 acquired a new deck. From June 1955 to December 1956, workmen dredged the harbor, broke up and removed existing concrete, laid rebar, and poured new concrete using hand trucks—lots and lots of hand trucks. Reconstructing the pier—the only one at the Charlestown Navy Yard capable of berthing an aircraft carrier—was part of the 1948 master plan intended to modernize the yard. [BOSTS-8784]

After winning an order to construct its first major steel vessel, the supply ship USS *Bridge* (AF-1), the Navy Yard extensively renovated Shipways 1. Taken on the day the keel was laid for *Bridge*, this photograph shows four hammerhead cranes that were installed to assist in the movement and placement of materials used in ship construction. To the left is the Electrical Shop (Building 103), in the background is the Forge Shop (Building 105), and to the right is the Shipfitters and Sheet Metal Shop (Building 104). During World War II, the harbor side of Building 104 was torn down to make way for a second shipways. [BOSTS-10536]

Four
MEMORIES OF THE YARD

Members of the Jemez tribe of Native Americans perform on the shipyard mall as part of the 1950 Red Feather Campaign, which raised money for charitable institutions. Tribe members were in Boston as part of Gene Autry's Rodeo Show, then appearing at Boston Garden. [BOSTS-7510]

Employees of the Supply Department participate in a recruitment parade during 1918. The sign on the truck urges people to go to the British and Canadian Recruiting Mission at 44 Bromfield Street, Boston, and join the forces in France. These views were taken on Ninth Street, between the Central Power Plant (Building 108) and the Supply Department (Building 149). [BOSTS-9911]

When the United States entered World War I, the Navy seized a number of German passenger liners in American ports for use as troop transports. USS *Leviathan* (Id. No. 1326), formerly SS *Vaterland*, was a regular visitor to the Navy Yard from 1917 to the mid-1920s. In the view above, troops bound for France crowd the ship's deck in September 1918. The war would be short for these men, for on November 11, 1918, an Armistice was declared. [BOSTS-11781]

In this night view, *Leviathan* occupies Dry Dock 3 in South Boston, after its release from naval service. [BOSTS-11772]

In May 1935, following his Second Antarctic Expedition, Admiral Richard E. Byrd arrived in Boston to a hero's welcome. Byrd's two ships, *Bear of Oakland* and *Jacob Rupert*, docked at the Navy Yard. Seen tied up at Pier 2, *Bear of Oakland* was ideal for icy waters. It had been used to rescue Lt. Adolphus W. Greely after his failed Arctic expedition in 1884 and, as *Bear*, it had served the Coast Guard in Alaskan waters for nearly 40 years. [BOSTS-10391]

Although Byrd's expedition was not an official Navy project, the service allowed him to store equipment in Building 34 at the yard. A rather disorganized array of material can be seen in this 1936 view. [BOSTS-9341]

Mrs. Cora L. Bennett Hoffman stands in reflection prior to the launching of USS *Bennett* (DD-473) on April 16, 1942. As sponsor, Mrs. Hoffman christened the destroyer named in honor of her late husband, Aviation Machinist Floyd Bennett. Bennett achieved distinction for his service with Admiral Byrd on the first flight over the North Pole. [BOSTS-10423]

With a crew of 160 blacks and 44 whites, USS *Mason* (DE-529) was considered an experiment by the overwhelmingly white Navy. Commissioned at Charlestown on March 20, 1944, *Mason* made six voyages from the United States to England and to Oran, Algeria, without loss of crew or vessels under its protection. Signalmen Second Class Joseph W. "Jack" Davis and Moselle White pose here for what has become the signature image of *Mason*. With the way snow is clumped to their pea jackets, they were possibly throwing snowballs. [BOSTS-11925]

Opposite: The aftermath of Operation Torch, the November 1942 invasion of North Africa, is shown in this series of images. A Navy photographer recorded scenes around the Moroccan port of Casablanca, including the view at top of the partially sunken SS *Porthos*, with stacks resting on the edge of a pier. In the view in the middle, it is difficult to make out the battle damage at midships to USS *Hambleton* (DD-455), torpedoed on its portside. Towed to Casablanca for temporary repairs, which involved removal of a 40-foot section of the ship, *Hambleton* was then sent to the Charlestown Navy Yard for reconstruction. A little more than a year later, the reconstructed destroyer stands at bottom in a mid-war, two-toned paint scheme prior to its return to active duty. [BOSTS-15822, 11334]

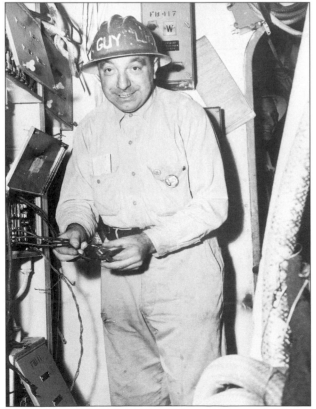

Throughout the 20th century, even at the height of wartime activity, the Navy Yard had an employees' band. Above, the band poses for its portrait in front of Building 107 in 1943. Among the band members is Guy Giarraffa, seen at left working as an electrician. Giarraffa led the band during the 1950s. [BOSTS-14957, 15804]

On February 3, 1943, the German submarine *U-233* torpedoed the Greenland-bound troop transport SS *Dorchester*. Of the 904 passengers and crew, only 229 were saved. A Catholic priest, a Jewish rabbi, and two Protestant clergymen were among the casualties, after they gave their life jackets to save four soldiers. On the tenth anniversary of the sinking, a symbolic reenactment occurred on USS *Constitution*. Army Chaplain James B. Allan, Father Edward J. Carney, Rabbi Joseph S. Shubow, and Army Chaplain Samuel Overstreet give life jackets to Sergeants Ludgere A. Dube, Clarke E. Richardson, Charles J. McCarthy, and Raymond A. Gignac. [BOSTS-7545]

During the 1950 Red Feather Campaign rally, Swedish movie star Marta Toren presents red feathers to George C. Tegan and Francis Repetto. [BOSTS-7510]

In return for appearing at the Red Feather rally, members of the Jemez tribe and other performers from the Gene Autry Rodeo Show were given a tour of the yard. [BOSTS-7702]

The crowning of a queen and the cutting of a cake—the 1950 sesquicentennial of the Charlestown Navy Yard was a time for celebration. At right, Mary Connelly, crowned Miss Sesquicentennial, waves to her subjects from the deck of a ship. Above, she is joined by Shipyard Commander Captain Richard M. Watt in cutting a cake as ladies-in-waiting Kathleen Roche and Marie Buckley look on. [BOSTS-7544]

In 1920, the obsolete battleship *Kearsarge* (BB-5) began a second career as a crane ship. Retaining the hull, the superstructure was reconfigured to support a crane and boom mechanism. Losing its original name to an aircraft carrier in 1941, *Crane Ship No. 1* (AB-1) served the Charlestown Navy Yard several times during its 35-year career. Contracted by a private salvage firm in September 1952, this relic of the "Great White Fleet" raised the trawler *Lynn* from the bottom of Boston Harbor. The trawler had sunk dramatically following a collision with the tanker *Ventura*; 15 men were lost. In this view, the deckhouse of *Lynn* breaks the surface. In the background is the tug *Juno*. [Jack Doherty, BOSTS-11628]

Navy truck 96-07924 teeters precariously over the edge of Dry Dock 2 following a March 1957 accident. Curious shipyard workers gather. The large, white building in the left background is Building 198, a temporary structure built during World War II. [BOSTS-15698]

On August 19, 1955, as Hurricane Diane hit the area, Jack Doherty braved the storm to capture this image of a van driving through deep water on Second Avenue past the Muster House. In the background is the Marine Corps Administration Building (Building 136). [BOSTS-9320]

Allan R. Crite, a noted Boston artist, worked as a technical equipment illustrator in the Design Division. In addition to his technical work, Crite produced illustrations for the *Boston Naval Shipyard News* encouraging safety, energy conservation, and workspace organization and cleanliness. Two examples of his drawings appear here. [BOSTS-7100]

SCULLERY

MAKE SURE THERE ARE (4) FOUR CARTS OF TRAYS AND (2) TWO CARTS OF PLATES AT ALL TIMES

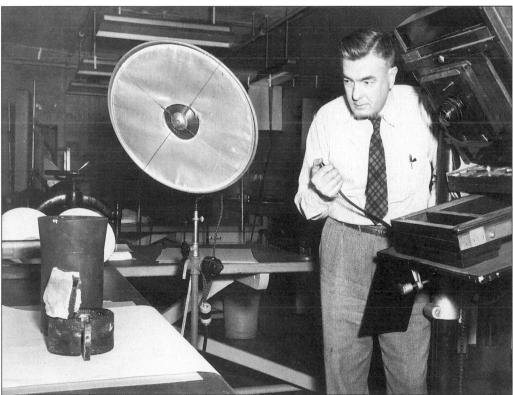

Howell Baldwin, the first supervisor of the Photo Lab, focuses a Deardorff studio camera on a sample in 1951. [BOSTS-7015]

25,000# HAMMER FOUNDATION, BLDG. #105. NOy-27 12
PART OF CONCRETE OBSTRUCTIONS ENCOUNTERED.
NY2-193(L)-1-53.

SOIL BEARING TEST FOR
25,000 LB. HAMMER. BLDG 105.   NY2-950(L)-3-53

In 1953 and 1954 the Navy installed a new 25,000-pound drop hammer in the Forge Shop (Building 105) for production of 4.75-inch chain for *Forrestal*-class aircraft carriers. Work began with excavations for the hammer's massive foundation and, as shown on the opposite page, involved clearing obstructions and testing soil strength. With the base in place, the hammer began to take its massive shape. Finally, on April 16, 1954, Mrs. Thomas Benton, below, christened the hammer "Monarch." To Mrs. Benton's left is Paul Ivas, the shop's master mechanic, and to her right is her husband, who chose the hammer's name and thereby won for his wife the privilege to christen it. [BOSTS-9709, 9710]

"Over 12,000 people ignored the threat of rain and turned out for the 6th Annual Shipyard Outing at Whalom Park, Fitchburg," reported the *Boston Naval Shipyard News* on September 3, 1953. A couple performs the Mexican Hat Dance. [BOSTS-7471]

In the 1960s, the Navy Yard celebrated Armed Forces Day in May with an Open House, which featured exhibits and demonstrations by the various shops. Above, "Willie the Welder" operates a "Spider Weldall" in 1967. On the following page, two scuba divers show off their skills in Dry Dock 1, while at bottom spectators watch a ropemaking demonstration. [BOSTS-7553; Nicholas Metta, BOSTS-7554]

Throughout the years, civic-minded yard workers participated in the larger Boston community by building floats for parades for patriotic or commemorative observances. In June 1949 the yard produced the above float celebrating industrial progress from 1800 through 1949 for the Bunker Hill Day parade and a parade celebrating Malden's 300th birthday. Thirteen years later, a model of USS *Constitution* was the centerpiece of a float in a parade on Evacuation Day (March 17, the day in 1776 when the British abandoned Boston). Where the flatbed connects to the truck cab stands a leprechaun, certainly intended for the holiday really being honored, St. Patrick's Day. [BOSTS-7631, 7633]

On August 18, 1972, retiring Shipyard Commander Rear Admiral Raymond Burk and his wife, Ramona, hosted an Apple Orchard Birthday Party in honor of the 172nd anniversary of the Navy Yard. The occasion doubled as their farewell, since Mrs. Burk wanted something different from the usual cocktail party. The couple stand next to a model of the shipyard in front of Quarters L-M-N-O (Building 266) at the lower (east) end of the yard. [Jack Doherty, BOSTS-7548]

BLDG. 39-3 MOVING CREW LOADING RACK
TRAILER FROM FIRE ESCAPE PLATFORM

Following the official closure of the Charlestown Navy Yard, a Boston Caretaker Group managed the Navy's final move from the yard and transfer of the property to the National Park Service and the Boston Redevelopment Authority. In May 1975 the two workers at left pause to smile for the photographer while removing furniture from the third floor of Building 39. They are standing on a trailer (below) that has been suspended from a crane over First Avenue, making their task easier. [BOSTS-9383]

MOVING CREW LOADING SUSPENDED TRAILER
FROM 3RD FLOOR FIRE ESCAPE PLATFORM
BLDG 39-3

Five
SERVING THE FLEET

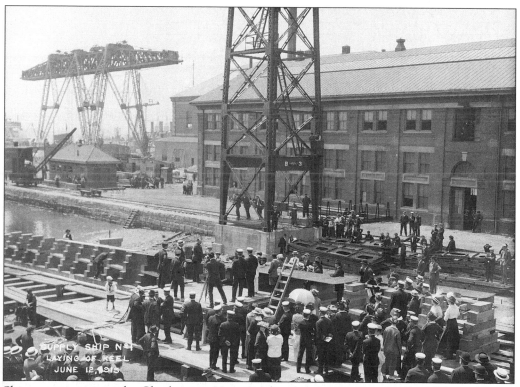

SUPPLY SHIP No 1
LAYING OF KEEL
JUNE 12, 1915

Ship construction at the Charlestown Navy Yard ended shortly after the Civil War, not to be resumed until the 1910s, when the yard fiercely contended for and won an order for construction of Supply Ship No. 1. To undertake this task, the yard extensively modernized Shipways 1, installing four hammerhead cranes. A photographer takes pictures as spectators gather at the shipways for the laying of the keel for USS *Bridge* (AF-1). The structure at center is the base of one of the cranes. The Electrical Shop (Building 103) is in the background, while the yard's 150-ton floating crane can be seen to the left. [BOSTS-10537]

Shipbuilders pose proudly in the midst of work on the keel of the recently begun USS *Neches* (AO-5). A chain suspended from a hammerhead crane supports a steel plate, while a forest of scaffolding outlines the shape of the future oiler's hull. [BOSTS-13738]

Workers prepare to cut steel plates for USS *Whitney* (AD-4) in the Plate Yard. [BOSTS-14687]

One month before commissioning, the deck of USS *Pecos* (AO-6) dances with workers. In the background to the left is the Electrical Shop (Building 103) and on the right is the Shipfitters, Plumbers, and Sheet Metal Shop (Building 104). Once again, Shipways 1 is a forest of scaffolding, with USS *Whitney* (AD-4) under construction. [BOSTS-13924]

Two workmen are dwarfed by the steam reciprocating engines being assembled for *Pecos* in the Machine Shop (Building 42) in 1921. [BOSTS-13925]

This 1939 view of the tug *Powhatan* (YT-128) was taken from a similar perspective to the waterfront view on the next page taken about 20 years earlier. Destroyers have replaced battleships; witness USS *Mayrant* (DD-402) docked by Pier 5. Behind *Mayrant* is Building 42 and the hammerhead cranes of Shipways 1. *Powhatan*, the centerpiece of this image, was completed by the yard in September 1938. [BOSTS-13985]

Images from two stereographs have been laid side-by-side to form a mini-panorama of the east end of the Navy Yard in the 1870s. At left are Building 42 and three shiphouses, while at right are moored the decommissioned hulls of *Ammonoosuc* and *Niagara*. The sterns of two frigates begun during the Civil War are poised on the building ways between the shiphouses for a launching that would never occur. [BOSTS-8978, 13773]

The basket masts of battleships dominate the Navy Yard waterfront in the late 1910s. In the background at left with a water tank on its roof is the Supply Department (Building 149), while Building 42 appears to the left of USS *Constitution*. The small round structure in front of Building 42 is the Pump House (Building 123), initially built for filling and draining Dry Dock 2 but later serving Dry Dock 1 as well. [BOSTS-8643]

On December 17, 1927, the submarine USS *S-4* (SS-109) sank with the loss of all hands after colliding with USCG *Paulding* (CG-17, ex-DD-22) off Cape Cod. Three months later, spectators watch solemnly as the salvaged submarine is floated into Dry Dock 2. Salvage pontoons including *YSP-6* and *YSP-10* stabilize the vessel. One positive result came from this disaster—the impetus for improvements in submarine rescue technology. [BOSTS-14138]

In the late 1920s, work began on the first of several extensive restorations of USS *Constitution*, the Navy's oldest commissioned vessel. Since the project was funded by a "Pennies Campaign" among schoolchildren, there was great public interest. Evelyn Williams, daughter of a yard officer at the time, recalled that on occasion her father would "ask me to take my little red wagon down to the wood shop" and get "a lot of little chips" from removed timbers to be mailed out as souvenirs to donors. This view of the bow shows the cradle that braced the weak hull while work was being done. The Riggers and Laborers Shop (Building 24) can be seen in the background. [BOSTS-10748]

Photographer Stanley P. Mixon prepares to make a trip by launch out to Presidents Roads in Boston's outer harbor to comply with Navy requirements that new and refitted ships be photographed against a neutral ocean background. The results of such a trip can be seen in the May 1940 view at the bottom of the opposite page of USS *O'Brien* (DD-415). [BOSTS-7716, 13816]

During the 1930s, Dry Dock 2 was used extensively for the construction of destroyers. USS *Walke* (DD-416) and USS *O'Brien* (DD-415) were laid down side-by-side on May 31, 1938. Some 11 months later, they are complete to their main deck. At their sterns are guides for the centerline of two more destroyers—USS *Madison* (DD-425) and USS *Lansdale* (DD-426)—laid down in December 1938. All four ships were floated (launched) on October 20, 1939, a task that required considerable skill to avoid the ships tipping over or hitting each other within the tight confines of the dock. [BOSTS-13817]

During World War II, the U.S. Navy would not allow women to work on board commissioned ships. Thus, most of them worked either on new ship construction or in shipyard shops. Here, women weld framing for the hull of USS *Trumpeter* (DE-279) on Shipways 2 in 1943. Hoses strewn about the framing connect to individual Hobart welding machines. [BOSTS-14958]

Shipyard employees gather at Dry Dock 1 as USS *Buck* (DD-420) is docked in August 1942, following a collision with SS *Atwatea* during convoy duty across the Atlantic. The destroyer's heavily damaged stern had to be cut away and allowed to sink in order to keep the ship afloat so it could be brought to the yard for repairs. [BOSTS-10578]

U.S.S. GILBERT ISLANDS (CVE-107)
STEPPING THE MAST.   NY2-825-5-52

Pride in workmanship helped motivate shipyard employees. Members of the Pipe and Woodworking Shops smile and wave as the mast of USS *Gilbert Islands* (CVE-107) is stepped in May 1952. [BOSTS-11234]

In these four views, USS *Antietam* (CVS-36) is brought into Dry Dock 3 for a routine hull inspection in 1955. Docking *Antietam* was a challenge, for the entrance to the dock was narrower than the dry dock itself; the aircraft carrier had only inches to spare. At left, sailors from the ship and shipyard workers help guide the ship to its proper position over the keel blocks on which it will rest once the dock is pumped dry. Above, the caisson closing the dock is being lowered into place. The imposing Boston Army Base rises behind *Antietam*. At right, workers prepare to make connections between shore utilities and the ship. [Stanley Mixon, BOSTS-10278]

From 1946 to 1955, the sloop-of-war USS *Constellation* was docked at the Charlestown Navy Yard along with USS *Constitution*. Because of the common but mistaken belief that the ship was the 1797 frigate of the same name built in Baltimore, rather than a totally new vessel built in Norfolk in the 1850s, a group in the Maryland city undertook to raise funds for its restoration. Since the century-old hull could not stand the stress of being towed to Baltimore, the Navy moved it there in a floating dry dock. In August 1955 the tugs *Chegodega* (YTB-542) and *Wawasee* (YTB-367) position the covered and demasted *Constellation* at the mouth of *ARD-16* for the long voyage south. *Constellation*, restored in the late 1990s to its true appearance as the Navy's last sail-only warship, occupies a place of pride in Baltimore's Inner Harbor. [BOSTS-10725]

CAISSON DD.#2

This dedicated shipyard worker stands in Dry Dock 2 next to a leaking caisson in August 1956. [BOSTS-15642]

By 1961, the Navy ordered a new caisson for Dry Dock 2 from a private shipyard in East Boston. In the progress view at right, two men watch idly as a welder installs a steel plate on the assembled frame. Pier 11 of the yard can be seen across the harbor, along with the approach to the Mystic-Tobin Bridge. The tall building in the background is Building 199. Above, the Ross Towboat Company tug *Sadie Ross* moves the completed caisson to Pier 3 at the mouth of the dock. The stacks of the Lincoln Wharf power plant of the Metropolitan Transit Authority, the flagpole of the Coast Guard Support Base, and the tower of the Customs House can be seen against the still-low Boston skyline in the background. [BOSTS-8837]

The last new ship built at the Charlestown Navy Yard was USS *Suffolk County* (LST-1173). Work began in the Mold Loft (Building 104) with production of templates for hull sections. Above, loftsmen lay out faring lines for hull sections, while below Bruce Nelson and Santo Passalacqua prepare templates for bilge plates. [Nicholas Metta, BOSTS-14317]

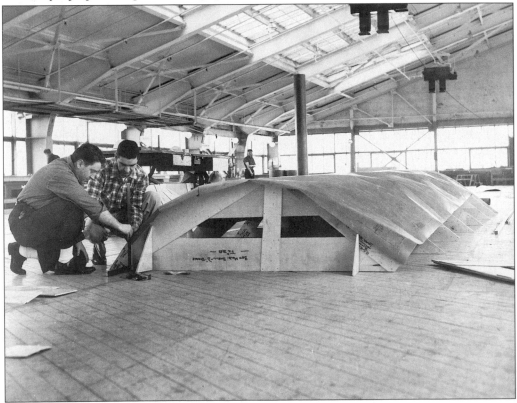

Nelson's and Passalacqua's work in the Mold Loft went to the Structural Shop (Building 195) for use in cutting steel plates. James Donovan, James Dwyer, Joseph Steinberg, and James Taylor clamp and fit a template to a steel plate in March 1955. [BOSTS-14317]

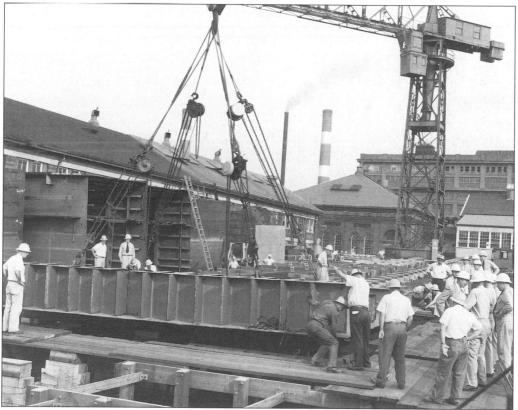

On July 15, 1955, workers laid the keel for *Suffolk County* on Shipways 1. John Chorba, with his left arm in the air, provides directions to the operator of the hammerhead crane as Wally Woods holds the end of a plate being set into place. [BOSTS-14328]

On September 5, 1956, Mrs. Mildred Miller O'Neill, wife of Congressman Thomas P. "Tip" O'Neill, Jr. (whose district included the Navy Yard), christened *Suffolk County*. Behind the christening party, spectators watch from the roof of Building 104. Shipyard Commander Rear Admiral William E. Howard assists Mrs. O'Neill, while Vice Admiral E.L. Cochrane, former chief of the Bureau of Ships, and Representative O'Neill (partially obscured) stand to the left. [BOSTS-14330]

USS SUFFOLK COUNTY LST-1173
PROGRESS PHOTO ASF-131-5-57

The newly installed bow doors are open and work is underway on the superstructure as *Suffolk County* sits at Pier 5. The tank-landing ship is just three months away from commissioning. [BOSTS-14324]

A welder works on the hull of *Suffolk County* in early 1956. [BOSTS-14320]

USS *Albany* (CA-123/CG-10) was the lead ship in a program to convert heavy cruisers to guided-missile ships, marrying World War II hulls with Cold War weaponry. Workers stream down double gangways at the stern of the ship during a surprise fire drill in May 1961. This image is a testament to the vast numbers of men employed during the conversion process. [BOSTS-10235]

By September 1962, *Albany*, tied up to Pier 4, appears as it would at the time of its recommissioning in November. [BOSTS-10186]

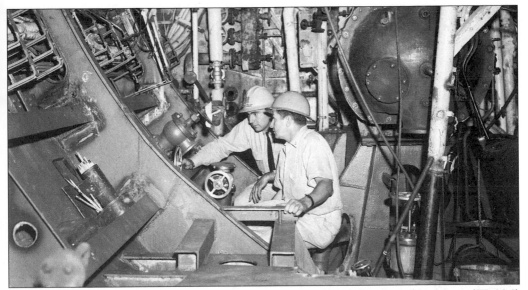

USS *Perry* (DD-844) was the first ship in the Fleet Rehabilitation and Modernization (FRAM) Program designed to prolong the life of World War II destroyers. In August 1959 ship liaison officer Lieutenant G.S. Langford and a worker confer in a boiler room. The insert in the lower view of the deck tracks the "Principal Dates" for the work. In the end, the ship was completed two months late, not bad for a prototype. [Nicholas Metta, Jack Doherty, BOSTS-13943]

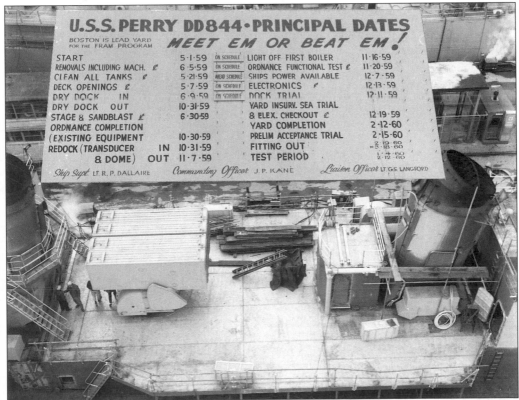

The Charlestown Navy Yard was a leader in development of sonar systems. Sonar domes on destroyers graduated from protrusions under the hull to bulbous domes incorporated into the bow. USS *Willis A. Lee* (DL-4) was used extensively to evaluate bow-mounted sonar. This view shows *Lee* in Dry Dock 2 in March 1961, after the bow had been removed in preparation for installation of a new experimental system. This dome is seen at right, suspended upside down from *YD-196* outside the caisson of Dry Dock 2 during testing for watertightness in May 1961. At the top of the next page, part of this unit is being removed in Dry Dock 4, in August 1965, so that another experimental unit can be installed. [Jack Doherty, BOSTS-14728, 14733]

In the early 1960s, the Navy decided to convert the *Forrest Sherman*-class all-gun destroyers of the mid-1950s into guided-missile ships. Due to fiscal constraints and problems with the Tartar missile system, only four were completed, including USS *Decatur* (DD-936/DDG-31). In March 1966 bridge cranes move a new afterstack for *Decatur* toward the door of the Boiler Shop (Building 106) for transport to the ship. Below, members of the Paint Shop apply the new hull number to the vessel. [Dennis Costin, BOSTS-10894, 10913]

Since the 1930s, and particularly after World War II, the Charlestown Navy Yard was known as a "destroyer yard." To exemplify this aspect of the yard's history for visitors, the National Park Service in 1978 obtained USS *Cassin Young* (DD-793) from the Navy. The ship arrived exhibiting corrosion and weathering from having been in "mothballs" since its decommissioning in April 1960. This is clearly visible in the view of the torpedo tubes and a 5-inch gun mount above. The shed on the stern in the view at right is part of the internal ventilating and dehumidifying system used to preserve the interior spaces of inactive vessels. Following restoration, which was carried out in Dry Dock 1, the ship was opened to visitors in June 1981. [Blaise Davi, National Park Service]

USS *Cassin Young* (DD-793) was no stranger to the Navy Yard, having undergone reconstruction and overhaul there throughout the 1950s. Except by accident, however, yard photographers did not document the ship's visits—the work done, while extensive, was no different from that being done on numerous other destroyers at the time. During the commissioning ceremony for the minesweeper USS *Vital* (MSO-474) on June 9, 1955, *Cassin Young*'s bold hull number appears in the background. [BOSTS-14561]

Six

YARD PLANS

Above: Kids play on an anchor in front of the tennis courts during Armed Forces Day celebrations in 1967. [BOST-7553]

Plans of the Charlestown Navy Yard from 1893, 1937, and 1963 on the following pages show the evolution of the site during the period covered by this book. On the earliest plan, the original west-to-east, north-to-south numbering of buildings and other major features is still largely intact. Thereafter, numbers were assigned as new facilities were added, principally in the late 1890s and early 1900s (buildings numbered in the 100-135 range), during World War I (numbers up to 185), and during World War II (through number 218). The late 1950s witnessed a final expansion of the numbering system when features such as flagpoles and light towers, heretofore unnumbered, were added to the list. A key to the location of specific buildings and structures mentioned in this book appears on p. 128.

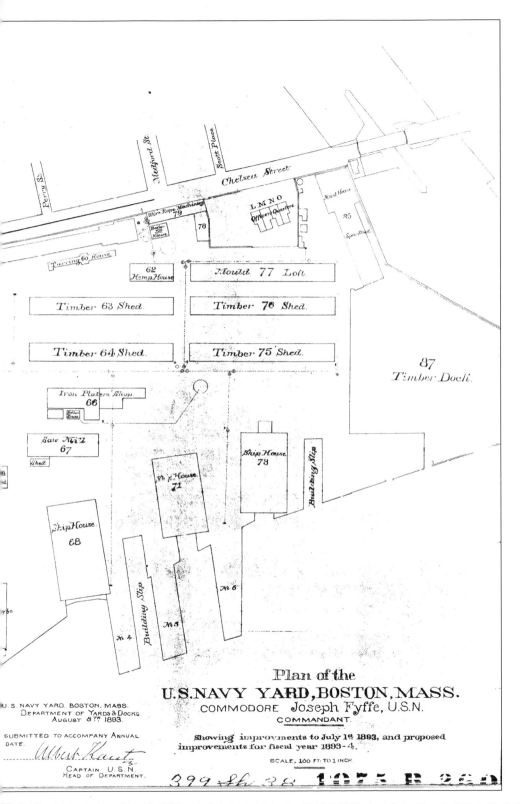

Plan of the
U.S. NAVY YARD, BOSTON, MASS.
COMMODORE Joseph Fyffe, U.S.N.
COMMANDANT.

Showing improvements to July 1st 1893, and proposed
improvements for fiscal year 1893-4.

SCALE, 100 FT. TO 1 INCH.

U.S. NAVY YARD, BOSTON, MASS.
DEPARTMENT OF YARDS & DOCKS.
AUGUST 8TH 1893.

SUBMITTED TO ACCOMPANY ANNUAL
DATE.

Albert Kautz

CAPTAIN U.S.N.
HEAD OF DEPARTMENT.

399 Sh 38 1075 B 260

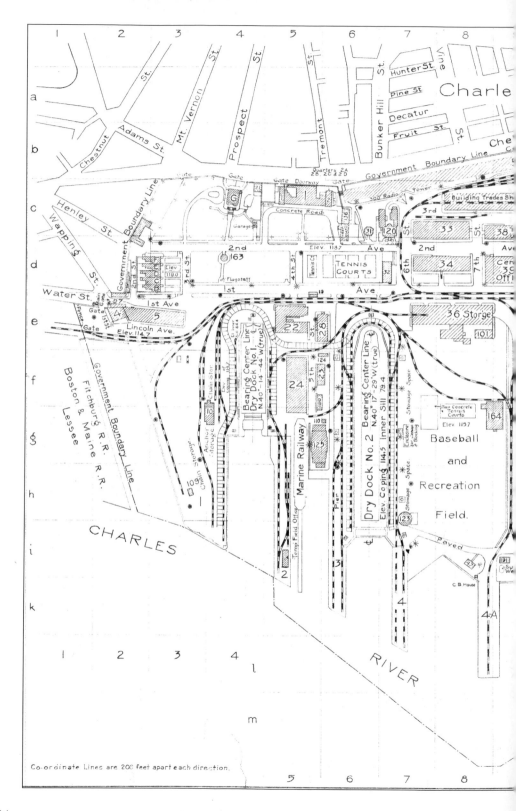

Co-ordinate Lines are 200 feet apart each direction.

124